MW01132278

Low Risk Investing
in
Florida Tax Certificates

How to Make Money
with
Florida Taxes

JODI HOCKINSON

Low Risk Investing
in
Florida Tax Certificates:
How to Make Money with Florida Taxes

ISBN: 9781888141665

Published by:

Southeast Media Productions
Carlisle, Pennsylvania
USA
(386) 503-6832
semediapro.com

Table of Contents

INTRODUCTION

Let's begin this by saying, please don't put all of your eggs in one basket! No system of investing or making money is perfectly safe. There are always risks involved in everything you do.

In fact, we will actually discuss some of the disadvantages as well as advantages of investing with Florida property tax. That being said, investing in Florida property tax certificates can be a low risk investment with a good to high return, especially compared to the return on a savings account or certificate of deposit.

Covered in our discussion will be the two different ways of investing, which are tax deeds and tax certificates. We will also discuss how a tax certificate sale works, the life of a tax certificate, applying for tax deed, how your investment works for you, how county held tax certificates work, online sales versus public auctions attended in person, and choosing the right certificates to bid on.

Also discussed are advantages and drawbacks for tax certificates, as well as tax deed sales.

You will receive a basic knowledge about how investing and returns work on this lower-risk, higher yield type of investment.

1

2 DIFFERENT WAYS OF MAKING MONEY WITH FLORIDA TAXES

There are two different ways to make money with Florida taxes. One is to purchase tax certificates, the other is to purchase property by way of a tax deed sale. Purchasing tax certificates is typically done for a calculated return on an investment.

The purchaser is not buying the property, but rather investing in the tax bill amount of the property. Purchasing property at a tax deed sale is an actual purchase of the property itself.

Investors at a tax deed sale can often purchase property at an amount much lower than the actual value of the property, which can then be built on or sold at a later date. Both tax certificate sales and tax deed sales are conducted by each individual county in Florida, and must comply with Florida statutes.

2

HOW DO FLORIDA PROPERTY TAXES WORK?

On November 1 of each year, tax bills are sent out, by county tax collectors, to Florida property owners.

Property tax is billed by the county, and can be comprised of ad valorem taxes as well as non ad valorem assessments. Ad valorem, meaning at value, is based on the value of the property.

The average ad valorem tax in Florida is about $25 per thousand dollars of the assessed value, also referred to as 25 mills.

Non-ad valorem assessments can also be assessed to certain properties, for different reasons such as waste disposal and district development.

Non ad valorem assessments can either have a flat fee per parcel, or based on unit value, such as the amount of front footage.

Assessed property values are determined by the county property appraiser's office each year, and are based on an assortment of criteria from the previous year, such as improvements, comparable sales and property condition.

Some tax bills have exemptions applied, most typically for homestead properties.

Florida taxes are billed in arrears. In other words, the tax bill that is sent out November 1 of 2018 would be for the 2018 taxes.

Tax bills that are paid early receive the benefit of a discount. For example, bills that are paid in November will receive a 4% discount, December a 3% discount, and so on, until March, when the actual amount of the bill is due.

Tax Bills do not become delinquent until April 1st of the following year. Upon April 1st, a 3% late penalty is applied.

At some point, usually during the month of May, unpaid taxes, along with the date and time of a tax certificate sale, are advertised in a local newspaper for three consecutive weeks.

Tax certificate sales are usually held on or about June 1st. Any taxes that remain unpaid at this point, with the exception of certain bills that are not eligible for tax certificate sale, are sold as tax certificates. Tax certificates that are not purchased at the annual sale are available for purchase throughout the year until they are sold.

Upon the sale of a tax certificate, a tax bill increases by about 11%. At this point, the property owner is not in danger of losing the property, until 2 years from the day that a tax bill becomes delinquent.

Once a bill has become 2 years delinquent, the certificate holder can apply for tax deed. This application forces a public sale of the land. Tax deed sales are conducted throughout the calendar year, depending on when they are applied for.

Tax certificates may be redeemed at any time up until the moment that a tax deed sale has occurred, and payment for that sale has been received by the clerk's office.

To redeem a tax certificate, the delinquent bill, including all fees, interest and penalties, would simply need to be paid at the Tax Collector's Office.

3

WHAT ARE TAX CERTIFICATE SALES?

Every year, each Florida County must determine a budget, which is dependent upon collection of property taxes.

A county's budget can include emergency services, law enforcement, road maintenance and even schools. The state recognizes that these budgets must be met, and has therefore set guidelines in order to help counties meet their budget when taxes are not paid.

One incentive to ensure that annual taxes are paid is the discount program. Property owners who pay their taxes each year can receive a discount of up to 4%, depending on how early the bill is paid.

When a tax bill remains unpaid, the budget still must be met. Therefore, tax collectors are required by Florida statute to conduct an annual tax certificate sale in order to help meet the county's budget.

In order to receive the amount due for delinquent tax bills, certificates are sold in the form of primary liens against the property. Those purchasing tax certificates are entitled to a return on their investment. These tax certificates are the main topic of this publication.

4

WHAT IS A TAX CERTIFICATE?

A tax certificate is your investment in a delinquent real estate tax bill. It is considered a first lien on property. As a certificate holder, you do not have any rights to the real estate itself.

In fact, when you become a certificate holder, you are prevented, by Florida statute, from even contacting the property owner until the given tax bill has become two years delinquent.

However, you will be able to force a tax deed sale on the property once the bill has become 2 years delinquent. Tax certificates are sold once a year by public auction (usually around June 1st), and then throughout the year for the certificates that did not sell at the auction and were struck to the county.

A tax certificate is purchased only for one year's delinquent taxes. There can be up to seven tax certificates on one property (one for each unpaid year).

When you bid at a tax certificate sale, you actually bid not on the amount of the tax bill, but on the amount of interest you are willing to take as a return on your money.

Therefore, bidding starts at the maximum, 18%, and goes downward in increments of ¼%, until there is a winning bid. You, as the winning bidder of a tax certificate, will make your purchase in the amount of the face value of the certificate.

The face value includes the bill itself, plus the 3% delinquent penalty that was applied on April 1, plus a 5% tax collector's fee, plus an additional 1.5% penalty if the sale begins in June, plus any other fees, such as advertising.

To become the purchaser of a tax certificate, you must be the winning bidder at the public tax certificate sale, or purchase a county-held tax certificate that has already been struck to the county, which we will discuss next.

It is always a good idea to be choosy about the tax certificate you purchase, as you may end up with the property at a later date.

5

COUNTY HELD TAX CERTIFICATES

Certificates that do not sell at the tax certificate sale are automatically struck off to the county, and can be purchased after the sale at 18% interest.

There are a number of advantages to purchasing a county-held certificate. First, you receive the maximum percentage return, 18%, on your investment. In addition, you can purchase a certificate on a tax bill that is already 2 years delinquent, and therefore can immediately apply for tax deed.

One thing to look out for, however, is a property that already has several county-held certificates (from previous years' unpaid taxes), especially if there are other properties in the surrounding area with the same situation. This could indicate that this property is not buildable, and therefore not a property that it would benefit you to end up with.

6

HOW DO YOU GET PAID WHEN A TAX CERTIFICATE IS REDEEMED?

Anyone can redeem a tax certificate, simply by paying the delinquent tax bill at the tax collector's office. The tax collector then disburses the funds to you, the certificate holder.

This means you do not have to hunt down the property owner for payment. In fact, Florida statute prevents certificate holders from contacting the property owner until after the bill has become 2 years delinquent. Tax certificates can be redeemed at any time after the certificate sale and before a tax deed sale has occurred, and payment has been received at the clerk's office.

7

LIFE OF
A TAX CERTIFICATE

Tax certificates have a life of seven years. If your tax certificate becomes 7 years old without being redeemed or tax deed application being made, the tax certificate becomes null and void.

As a tax certificate holder, you must make application, if your tax certificate has not been redeemed, before it is too late! It sounds simple to *plan* to make application for tax deed, but it is important to *plan in advance.*

When you make application, you must redeem all other outstanding tax bills. So, a property that you have planned to invest in the amount of one tax certificate could cost you up to seven or eight outstanding tax bills just to prevent your original investment from disappearing as per the statute of limitations.

Therefore, it is vital that you research outstanding tax bills on any certificate you purchase, and then keep an eye on the following tax years to make sure that once you apply for tax deed, if necessary, you will be able to afford to do so.

8

TAX CERTIFICATE SALE - HOW BIDDING AND PERCENTAGES WORK

Tax certificate auctions can be held online or in person, depending on the individual county in which they are held. Tax certificates are sold to the bidder willing to take the smallest investment return on the value of a given certificate.

Tax certificates are purchased by the winning bidder at face value, which is the sum of the amount due in delinquent taxes, plus advertising fees, times a 5% tax collector's fee.

Bidding begins at 18% and proceeds downward in increments of ¼%. The winning bid can be as low as 0%. You can bid whatever minimum amount that you feel comfortable with.

Provided the winning bid is not 0%, the certificate holder is guaranteed a return of at least 5% of the face value of a tax certificate. For example: You are the winning bidder of a tax certificate with a face value of $100.00. Your winning bid was 2%. You will pay the face value of the certificate immediately.

Even though your winning bid was only 2% per annum, you are still guaranteed a minimum of 5% return on your investment. If the property owner redeems the certificate by paying the bill the next day, you will receive $105.00 back.

Figured at an investment that only lasted, say, one month before you have received your redemption check, you have received an annual percentage rate of 60% on your investment.

Bidders are often required to register in advance for a tax certificate sale, and usually required to place a deposit in the amount of 10% of what they intend to spend.

If you are bidding in an online sale, you can place as many bids as you like, but your purchasing power may be cut off as soon as the purchase amount, based upon your deposit amount, has been reached.

Although all counties are required to conduct tax certificate sales in accordance with Florida statutes, the manner in which each county tax certificate sale proceeds may differ from one county to the next.

For example, a public sale that is not held online may involve the sale of one tax certificate at a time until every certificate is either sold or struck off to the county. This process can take days.

An online sale may be conducted consecutively by each individual parcel as well, or it may be conducted in groups called batches. At a public sale, not online, the highest possible bid is still 18%, and bids still go downward in increments of $\frac{1}{4}$%.

The winning bidder is the one who bids the lowest percentage amount. That winning bidder must then cash out by paying the actual face value of the certificate. If the winning bidder fails to pay for the certificate, the deposit is forfeited, and the certificate must be resold.

Online sales can differ in a variety of ways. For example, the deadline date for making a deposit may differ. The sale date itself may differ. The amount of parcels per batch may differ. The cutoff time or date for bidding may differ.

Counties may also choose to handle the manner of bidding differently. For example, some counties with online sales will allow bidders to enter a "minimum bid" This is called proxy bidding (this would be the equivalent to placing a bid on e-bay).

About one half of online tax certificate sales offer proxy bidding. This manner would allow the county's system to automatically bid against other bidders in your behalf until the winning minimum bid amount has been reached.

Some counties allow bidders to place one bid only, which can be any amount from zero to 18%. These bids are placed blindly without any knowledge of what amounts others might bid.

In addition, counties may allow companies to register multiple times, with one parent company and up to hundreds of subordinate companies. This is for a very good reason.

Let's say you have placed your bid at the lowest possible interest rate that can result in a return, $\frac{1}{4}\%$. Suppose you do this and so do several other bidders. How is it decided which one is the winning bidder?

In a public, in-person sale, the auctioneer would be forced to decide who placed that bid first. In a computerized auction, when bids are tallied in batches, the winning bidder would be decided by the computer at random.

If you have hundreds of companies placing a bid at $\frac{1}{4}\%$ against, say 2 dozen bidders, the likelihood of one of your companies being awarded the winning bid is substantially increased.

However, you must watch out for how deposits are treated with subsidiary companies. In some county sales, the deposit placed by the parent company may be used by any of the subsidiaries until the purchase amount has been reached. In some sales, the deposit amount could apply only to the entity that placed the deposit.

9

BIDDING
ZERO PER CENT

The lowest possible bid on a tax certificate is 0%, but this bid is usually not placed, as bidding 0% means there is no return on your investment- not even the 5% minimum. In order to receive the 5% minimum return on your investment, you must bid at least ¼%.

Examples of investors who would be served by bidding 0% include mortgagees who need to protect their interest in the property but do not want the tax bill to be ever increasing, or family members that have helped to pay the tax bill but need protection for their interest in the property.

Loaning someone money to pay taxes can be risky, but if you purchase a tax certificate at 0%, you might not receive a return, but the property cannot be sold free of encumbrances without the taxes being redeemed.

It might also not be a risk or trust issue but for financial protection, such as the case of the owner passing away. There might be a battle over who owns the property, but it will be clear as to who a certificate holder is.

10

ARE TAX CERTIFICATES CONSIDERED LIQUID ASSETS?

Tax certificates are not considered liquid assets. However, tax certificates can be transferred.

If you own a tax certificate and would like to cash out by selling it to a third party, simply contact the tax collector's office for that county to obtain a transfer form. The fee for a transfer of certificate ownership is $2.25.

11

WHY A LOW PERCENTAGE BID IS STILL A GOOD INVESTMENT

The lowest possible bid that can be made on a tax certificate is actually 0%, but then there is no return on your investment. The lowest possible bid to make and still receive a return on your investment is ¼%.

How could you possibly make money on such a low bid? Here's how! As long as you don't bid 0%, you are guaranteed a minimum return of 5% upon redemption.

So even if the certificate is redeemed the next day, you will receive a 5% return on your money! And you don't need to do anything to get it, besides sit back and wait for your redemption check to arrive from the tax collector's office.

If your certificate is redeemed the first month, you have made a 60% annual percentage rate on your investment! But that's not all- it gets better! Even if it takes 2 years for the owner to pay his taxes, you still receive at least 2½% per annum on your money. I said, "at least," because once the tax bill itself becomes 2 years delinquent, at this point your certificate is only about 22 months old, you can force a tax deed sale.

From the time you apply for tax deed, you begin to receive 18% per annum on your tax certificate investment, tax deed application fees and the redemption of any other outstanding taxes.

In fact, there are investment companies that hire college students to participate in sales, bidding as low as ¼%, just so that they can wait out the 22 months and increase the total average percentage.

In effect, your interest amount of at least 2½% per year has just leaped up to 18% per year- that's 1.5% per month from the time you apply for tax deed until everything is redeemed, or the property sells at tax deed sale.

So, 5% for 22 months begins at about 2¾% per annum, plus the first month's interest after tax deed application brings it up to about 3⅓% per year. The next month brings it up to about 3¾% per year on your return, and so on.

Before you know it, your return has not only met what you might have made in a CD or in your savings account, it has exceeded that return by far. And the beauty of the whole thing is that the 5% initial return was only on the certificate. You don't even have to invest more until it's time to collect 18% on your money!

If the tax certificate is redeemed before tax deed application is made, the investor is still ahead, because the interest that has been earned is still greater than the amount you can typically get from a savings account or CD.

12

COUNTY HELD CERTIFICATES-18%

When a tax certificate does not sell, it is "struck off" to the county, and becomes a county held tax certificate. County held tax certificates are struck off at 18% per annum, and can be purchased at face value over the counter, or on line (depending upon the particular county's procedures) after the sale. County tax certificates can be purchased all year round.

The face value of the tax certificate equals the face value at the time of the sale, any added fees, plus the interest that has accrued since the sale. Your interest begins at a minimum return of 5%, then accrues at 1½% per month against your face value.

This means that even if a tax certificate is redeemed the next month, you will receive not just 1½% on your investment, you will receive the minimum, which is 5%.

Once the property tax bill connected to this tax certificate becomes 2 years delinquent, you can apply to force a tax deed sale. So, technically, you could purchase a county held tax certificate that is at least two years old and apply the next day for the tax deed sale.

13

BIDDING ONLINE VS. GOING IN PERSON TO THE SALE

There is a great deal to be said about choosing online auctions. The advantages include lowered travel expenses, being able to bid remotely from the comfort of your home, being able to determine, in advance, the amount of money you wish to spend, and keeping to that amount. Your online deposit will determine your maximum spendable amount, and once that amount is reached, you will not be able to go higher.

However, there are distinct advantages to choosing a sale that is held on site, in person. A great advantage is that the large companies that are bidding online are not as likely to have representatives, or as many representatives, at an in-person sale.

Fewer people will be bidding on certificates. Fewer bidders will equate to less capital to spend, which means the interest rates for winning bidders will be higher.

14

CHOOSING THE CERTIFICATES TO BID ON, AND PLANNING WISELY

One thing you will want to look for is certificates on property that already have at least one year in delinquency, which means there is an older tax certificate in place on that property. This is because the certificate holder of that tax bill will need to apply for tax deed before the certificate becomes 7 years old and the tax bill remains unpaid.

That certificate holder would have to apply for tax deed before that point, or he will lose his investment. When the certificate holder applies for tax deed, all outstanding tax bills must be paid, which means that your certificate will need to be redeemed. This also means there will be no efforts expended on your part, just depositing the check once you receive it from the tax collector's office.

Purchasing a tax certificate on a property that already has a county-held certificate can be a real plus. Counties are required by Florida statute to apply for tax deed on properties that are at least $5,000 in assessed value, so there is less likelihood of the bill dropping off by virtue of the statute of limitations.

Avoid properties with too many tax certificates. See if surrounding properties all have outstanding delinquent bills. This could indicate that the property in question is not buildable. At the very least, you would have to pay all of the outstanding tax bills in order to force a tax deed sale.

When deciding which county to look into the purchase of tax certificates, try the counties that are the fasted growing. According to a US Census report released in 2008, Florida counties included in the top 100 fastest growing were Washington, Sumter, Flagler, and Wakulla Counties. And don't forget the fastest growing metropolitan statistical areas, which included Palm Coast and Ocala.

The object of investing in tax certificates is to plan for a winning situation no matter what the outcome. If the tax certificate you purchase is redeemed quickly, you are ahead, because you have received a higher return on your investment.

If is redeemed at any time before you can apply for tax deed, you are ahead, because you still receive a 5% minimum return, no matter how short a time period has gone by.

If your certificate is not redeemed and you apply for tax deed, you are ahead, because your return jumps up to 18% per year until the date of the sale. If no one bids at the tax deed sale, and the property does not have homestead exemption, you are ahead, because you have become a property owner. Plan for a winning situation by being prepared to handle any eventuality. Examples of planning include:

1. Choosing the property wisely with the understanding that you may end up with it one day.

2. Be prepared to spend money to make money. If you apply for tax deed, you will need to have enough money to redeem all outstanding taxes in addition to application and title search fees.

Moreover, if you apply for tax deed on a property with homestead exemption, the minimum bid will be your total investment plus one half of the assessed value of the property.

If you are not prepared to pay that amount at the public sale, you might be stuck, at least temporarily, with no return on your investment. If there is no bidder, you will neither receive the property nor any money. The property will be placed on the list of lands available, with the county clerk's office.

3. Be prepared for a certificate to be redeemed just before it is time to apply for tax deed. There won't be 18% returns in the future of this bill, but you will receive the liquidity you need to reinvest.

4. Don't count your chickens before they hatch- Keep an eye on the properties attached to your certificates and be prepared to buy future certificates on the same property.

5. If you purchase a certificate at a higher amount, such as the maximum at 18%, you may not want to apply for tax deed right away. Your investment, after all, is accruing at a phenomenal interest rate.

In fact, if someone purchases a certificate on the next year's taxes, for example, but at a very low rate such as ¼ %, they will be more likely to apply for tax deed as soon as that bill becomes 2 years delinquent.

That way, their tiny interest rate will jump to 18%. The best part is, *they* will have to redeem all outstanding tax bills to apply for tax deed, which means your tax certificate will be redeemed and you will receive your redemption check.

Researching outstanding tax bills can often be done online with the individual county's tax collector website. Assessed values can be researched with the county appraiser's office, which can also often be done online.

Research for outstanding liens that would not be forgiven at a tax deed sale, such as IRS tax liens, can be done through the county clerk's office, which, in addition, can often be done online.

15

CAN A TAX CERTIFICATE BE CANCELLED BY THE COUNTY?

Yes. When a tax certificate is cancelled by the county due to an error made by the tax collector, property appraiser or any other county or municipal official, the certificate holder will receive an 8% return on his investment, OR the amount that was bid at the tax certificate sale, whichever is less. This amount is calculated beginning the date of the sale until the date the refund is ordered.

16

WHEN YOU CAN APPLY FOR TAX DEED - AND WHAT HAPPENS WHEN YOU APPLY

Once the tax bill that your tax certificate represents has become 2 years delinquent, you may apply for tax deed. This time frame can be crucial, especially if your winning bid was as low as ¼%.

The longer you wait, the smaller interest rate your investment will accrue. To apply for tax deed on a property, you, as the certificate holder, would submit an application along with fees for title search and clerk's procedures, such as serving the property owner(s).

You also must pay all other outstanding tax bills that are due on the property. This can come to a substantial amount if there are several delinquent bills due on the property.

The good news is that once you make application, you begin to earn 18% per annum for not only the original amount, but all of the fees and redemptions that were incurred in order to apply for tax deed. Your investment will continue to accrue interest until the actual tax deed sale, which is scheduled by the clerk's office.

Once the funds are received by the winning bidder at a tax deed sale, all monies received are disbursed to the primary lien holders first, such as property taxes and IRS liens, then to other lien holders. If there are any funds left after all liens have been paid, the remainder would go the property owner. With the exception of certain liens, such as IRS liens, all outstanding liens will be forfeited.

17

PURCHASING PROPERTY BY TAX DEED SALE

Tax deed sales are conducted by the county clerk, and are held periodically throughout the year, based upon tax deed applications that are submitted. Properties sold by tax deed sale can be purchased for a significantly lower amount than the assessed value of the property.

However, please be aware that not all liens are forgiven upon a sale by tax deed. For example, government liens, such as outstanding taxes and IRS liens, must be paid in order to obtain clear title on the property.

Tax deed sales are held by public auction, usually in person. The minimum bid is typically, but not always, including all outstanding real estate taxes due on the property being sold.

Many outstanding liens are forgiven at a

tax deed sale, but government liens and outstanding taxes are not. Because of this, it is important to search for outstanding liens on a property when planning to bid at a tax deed sale.

For example, there could be IRS liens in place, which can usually be found by conducting a search of the county clerk's public records. There could also be outstanding property taxes that were omitted from the tax deed application, such as a tax bill that becomes due after the application has already been made.

During the tax deed application process, all interested parties, such as mortgage holders, that are found in a required title search, are notified. They therefore have the opportunity to either stop the tax deed process by paying the outstanding taxes due, or to actually show up at the tax deed sale to bid on the property itself.

It is up to the interested parties to protect their investment, or interest, in the property by taking one of these actions.

A tax deed sale can be stopped at any time, by anyone, prior to the tax deed sale and payment to the clerk's office, simply by redeeming the outstanding property taxes.

So, technically, a tax deed sale could take place, and the whole process could be cancelled if the property taxes are redeemed before the money is collected for the sale.

If you are the winning bidder at a tax deed sale, it may be necessary to sue for quiet title, which "quiets" any interest that may be perceived, and establishes your sole interest in the property.

That being said, you can still come out with a property even after all of your expenses, that you can sell for a nice profit.

When choosing a property to bid on at a tax deed sale, research the outstanding liens, such as IRS liens, that will not be forgiven at the sale, and current property taxes that are due, and will also need to be paid.

Be sure that the total amount you need to pay will be greatly outweighed by the assessed value of the property you are purchasing.

18

DRAWBACKS

Tax certificates are not considered a liquid asset, although they can be liquidated by transferring ownership. Another drawback is that you could wait up to seven years before the tax certificate is redeemed.

If you are not able to afford to pay all outstanding taxes when you make application for tax deed, you could lose your investment once the certificate becomes 7 years old and becomes void by virtue of the statute of limitations.

Once you force a tax deed sale, it is possible that there will be no bidders on the property. This means that the property would become yours. You will want to make sure that your entire investment does not exceed the actual value of the property.

If you force a tax deed sale on a property with homestead exemption, the minimum bid will include one half of the assessed value of the property. If no one bids at the sale, you will not receive the property, and you will not receive your redemption. The property will be placed on the list of lands available with the county's clerk of court.

Purchasing property by tax deed sale could be more of a risk, because of tax liens that might be in place. Not all liens are forgiven, such as IRS liens and outstanding tax bills that were not included in the application.

It might also be more difficult to obtain title insurance. Title searches are done during the application process for a tax deed sale, which will name different interested parties that must be notified of the impending sale.

The results of this title search can be found on public record with the county clerk's office. Tax Deed Sale purchases could also be a higher initial investment. Increased investment amount can result in an increased risk.

19

ADVANTAGES

Most certificates are redeemed quickly. Even tax certificates purchased at the lowest percentage realize a return of more than 2½% per annum at the very least.

This would be provided that you initiated a tax deed sale once the tax bill becomes 2 years delinquent, and also provided that the winning bid was not 0%.

Most liens of record are forgiven upon tax deed sale. Liens that are not forgiven include all government liens, such as tax bills and IRS liens.

20

GETTING STARTED

To get started purchasing your tax certificates, simply visit floridataxcollectors.com and click on local services provided to navigate to links to the assorted Florida tax collectors.

Many of these sites will offer rules and explanations for their tax certificate sale procedures. Although all counties must comply with Florida statutes, each county has its own procedures and policies.

Start by contacting one or two counties of your choice to ask how their tax certificate procedures work, whether sales are online or in person, and if it is possible to get a list of county-held certificates currently available for purchase.

It is not necessary to be a US citizen to purchase property or to participate in tax certificate sales. However, some counties may require you to have a United States federal ID number.

Many counties offer tax certificate sale information right on their websites. Questions you can ask to get started are:

- Is your tax certificate sale online or in person?

- How do I register for a sale?

- Do you require a deposit?

- How do I get a list of county held tax certificates?

21

CONCLUSION

You now have a basic knowledge of how tax certificates and tax deed sales work. We have discussed tax certificate sales and tax deed sales, including advantages, drawbacks, researching properties and how to get started with your investment. We hope you have enjoyed *How to Make Money with Florida Taxes*.

DISCLAIMER

This publication is intended to offer basic information about making a solid return with Florida property taxes. It is not all inclusive.

For exact details, current rules, statutes and fees, please contact a Florida Tax Collector's office, or refer to Florida Statutes, Chapter 197. This is not a get a "get rich quick" scheme.

Information and opinions expressed in this publication reflect the personal opinions of the author. Please consult your tax advisor prior to making any investment, tax certificate, tax deed, or otherwise.

The information offered is general knowledge based on Florida Statute that is designed to help you in your decision to make money by investing in Florida property tax.

ABOUT THE AUTHOR

Jodi Hockinson, BA, CFCA, DTR, CDM, CFPP, was born in Houston, Texas, in 1963. She holds degrees in social sciences/history, nutrition and liberal arts.

She was a long-time employee of a Florida county tax collector's office, and worked extensively with tax certificates and tax deed application

In addition to *Low Risk Investing*, she has written a number fiction and nonfiction books including special interest diet books for persons suffering from gout and ulcerative colitis.

.

57354586R00027